ITALY

Recipes, Flavors & Traditions

P.J. Tierney

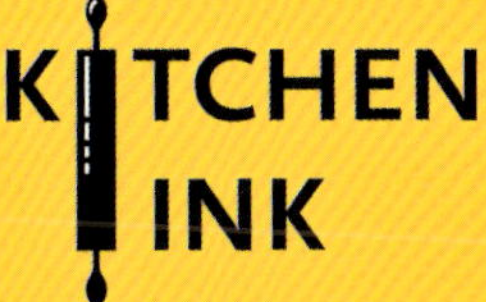

KITCHEN INK's passionate Kids in the Kitchen team of recipe creators, testers, editors, food stylists, photographers, and designers work tirelessly to create products that introduce kids to cooking. Having fun, making memories in the kitchen, and creating a delicious meal is what we are all about.

Our easy-to-follow, creative, and delicious recipes—kid-tested and parent-approved—include both healthy meals and special treats. Adult supervision and safety first are always important in the kitchen. We hope you enjoy our books as much as we have loved creating them.

Download a free culinary passport pdf. This passport has all pages; it does not contain the stickers found in the culinary passport sold with *The Global Cookbook, Delicious Recipes from Seven Continents.*
ISBN: 978-1-943016-22-8
www.kitcheninkpublishing.com

Recipes, text, and photographs by Kitchen Ink Publishing.

Publisher's Note
While every care has been taken in compiling the recipes for this book, neither Kitchen Ink Publishing, nor any other persons who have worked on this publication, can accept responsibility for any errors or omissions, inadvertent or not, that may be found in the recipes or text, nor for any problems that may arise as a result of preparing these recipes. If you have any special dietary requirements, restrictions, or medical conditions, it is advisable to consult a medical professional before following any of the recipes contained in this book.

Library of Congress Cataloging-in-Publication data is available.
ISBN 978-1-943016-27-3

First Edition
28 29 27 26 25 10 9 8 7 6 5 4 3 2 1

Printed in China

Kitchen Ink Publishing
114 John Street, #277
New York, NY 10038

Kitchen Ink books may be purchased for educational, business, or sales promotional use. For information, please email the Special Markets Department at sales@kitcheninkpublishing.com.

See what Kitchen Ink is up to, share recipes and tips, and shop our store—www.kitcheninkpublishing.com.

  kitcheninkpublishing

For Alexis
Your talent and creativity are inspiring.
Our Roman Holiday and culinary
adventures are at the top of my list.

Introduction by P.J. Tierney

On my first trip to Italy, I met my cousin Alexis, an architect in Rome. I was expecting a fabulous city tour, and she did not disappoint. Rome dates to 753 BC, but the title of the oldest city in Italy belongs to Matera, dating to 251 BC. Rome's Pantheon is the oldest Italian building still in use, built as a temple from 25 to 27 BC. The Pantheon is approximately 510 years older than the Colosseum; both are must-see.

Walking around Vatican City is fascinating, as is Saint Peter's Basilica, which has a breathtaking dome designed by Michelangelo. The frescoes on the ceiling, collectively known as the Sistine Ceiling, were commissioned by Pope Julius II in 1508 and painted by Michelangelo from 1508 to 1512. Read more about this treasured Italian artist on page 97.

I was looking forward to all the delicious food and wine we would enjoy. Italians eat a light meal for breakfast, colazione, around 7-9 am. Children will have warm milk, cereal, or a sweet treat. Adults enjoy an espresso with biscotti (recipe page 4) or pastry.

Usually, a dessert is eaten for breakfast, and you will find a delicious Ciambellone (bundt cake) on page 2 and a Panna Cotta recipe on page 18 for breakfast or dessert – you choose.

I always enjoyed watching my father dig into his Tartufo and the smile on his face when he got to the cherry in the middle; the recipe for this frozen dessert is on page 78. Other desserts included are delicious treats and for special occasions. Paul's and my wedding cake was Tiramisu and this traditional Italian recipe on page 94 is my favorite.

Italians' main meal is lunch, called pranzo. It usually lasts two hours, from 12:30 to 2:30 p.m., and often consists of multiple courses, a primo (pasta, soup, or a pasta dish) beginning with the colorful Antipasto Skewers, Risotto alla Milanese page 68 , a secondo such as the Chicken Marsala on page 42 and a contorno (side dish) like Roasted Vegetables (page 36).

I couldn't wait to try pizza in Italy; different regions in Italy have their own style of pizza. Pizza Romana is a delicious thin-crust pizza, while Naples is home to pizza napolitana with a soft, thin, bubbly crust, topped with marinara sauce and mozzarella. I've included a Caprese Pizza recipe on page 45 and make-your-own pizza sauce on page 45.

Dinner in Italy is typically eaten around 8 pm, and a family dinner could be over in an hour or less. Dinner is usually lighter than lunch to ensure a good night's sleep. Begin with Balsamic Bruschetta on page 26. Share a Big Night Salad on page 28, and Ricotta Gnocchi with Tomato Sauce on page 66.

This book is part of the Culinary Passport Series; when you complete Italian Wedding Soup, page 33, Homemade Pasta on page 50, and Crostoli on page 88 place the corresponding sticker in your culinary passport or mark the recipe to track your success and journey around the world through food.

Italians love celebrations, and 40 days before Easter, Carnevale begins—a party to eat, drink, and have fun before Lent's limitations. During the festival, Chiacchiere (recipe on page 88) is served; make this recipe and mark your Culinary Passport. Read more about Carnevale on page 99.

Preparing all the recipes in a book is challenging and will take time. You may want to pass on a recipe you think you may not like. You don't have to like every recipe, but make and taste it—you might be surprised. Once you complete all the recipes in the book, congratulations! Cross off the Italy book in your Culinary Passport. Quite the accomplishment!

P. J. Tierney

A Note from the Kids in the Kitchen Team

Each recipe notes the number of servings and the time needed to prepare the dish. 
Please note, the recommended chilling time for a dish may not be included in its active preparation time.

This cookbook includes easy recipes and those requiring a little more patience and skill. As you become more comfortable preparing recipes, it is important to be challenged and improve your kitchen skills.

An adult should be with you to assist, especially when using a knife and the stovetop, and when putting your delicious dishes into and bringing them out of the hot oven. It is up to the adult to decide when you can be more independent in the kitchen.

Step-by-step directions tell you what you need to prepare the dish. Read each recipe completely before you begin and make sure you have all the tools and ingredients you need. These recipes are written for kids all around the globe and both US measurements and metrics are included.

Sometimes a recipe may call for an ingredient you do not have. A substitution will be offered for an international ingredient that may be challenging to find. Please note that if an ingredient is marked "optional," you can leave it out of the recipe if you choose.

If you are vegetarian, you will find recipes without meat or with suggestions to prepare meatless versions of the dish.

Everyone is excited to taste the food they have created BUT, hit the brakes. Food is piping hot when removed from the oven. Always be patient and let the food cool before sampling. Your tongue will thank you.

Always clean up the kitchen when you are done and remember that more hands make light work. Have a cleanup party and everyone is rewarded with dessert.

Contents

Breakfast

Small Plates, Sides & Snacks

Entrées

Desserts

Breakfast

Ciambellone (Italian Bundt Cake)

1 hour

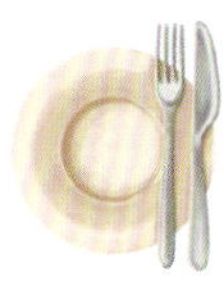
12 servings

Ingredients

5 eggs

½ cup (120 milliliters) sugar

Zest and juice from 2 lemons

1 cup (240 milliliters) vegetable oil

1 cup (240 milliliters) water

1 tablespoon (15 milliliters) vanilla extract

2 ½ cups (600 milliliters) flour, sifted

1 tablespoon (15 milliliters) baking powder

2 tablespoons powdered sugar for dusting

TIP

Drizzle the cooled cake with lemon glaze (recipe on page 10).

Directions

1. Preheat oven to 375°F (190°C), grease a bundt pan with oil, and lightly flour. Set aside.
2. In a large bowl, beat the eggs with the sugar until light and doubled in volume, about 3 minutes.
3. Add the zest, juice, oil, water, and vanilla and beat until mixed well.
4. In a medium bowl, mix the sifted flour with the baking powder. Slowly add to the egg mixture, mixing until well incorporated.
5. Bake for 35 to 40 minutes.
6. Allow the cake to cool before removing it from the pan and dusting it with powdered sugar.

Biscotti

45 minutes

20 Biscotti

Ingredients

1 ½ cups (360 milliliters) all-purpose flour

1 ½ teaspoons (7.5 milliliters) baking powder

¼ teaspoon (1.2 milliliters) salt

1 egg + 1 egg white

½ cup (120 milliliters) sugar

¼ cup (60 milliliters) coconut oil

½ teaspoon (2.5 milliliters) cinnamon

½ tablespoon (7.5 milliliters) orange juice

½ tablespoon (7.5 milliliters) orange zest

½ teaspoon (2.5 milliliters) vanilla extract

½ teaspoon (2.5 milliliters) almond extract

½ cup (120 milliliters) almonds, blanched

⅓ cup (80 milliliters) mini chocolate chips

TIP
Sift dry ingredients to prevent hard middles.

Directions

1. In a medium bowl, combine the flour, baking powder, and salt.
2. In a large bowl, add the egg, egg white, and sugar; mix to combine.
3. Beat in the oil, cinnamon, orange juice, zest, vanilla extract, and almond extract.
4. Add the flour mixture to the egg mixture and beat slowly until well blended.
5. Fold the almonds and chocolate chips into the cookie dough by hand.
6. Chill the dough in the refrigerator for 15 minutes.
7. Preheat oven to 350°F (180°C).
8. Form the dough into a 12-inch (30.5-centimeter) long mound.
9. Place the dough on a cookie sheet lined with parchment paper and bake for 25 minutes.
10. Allow the cookie to cool.
11. Carefully use a sharp serrated knife to separate the biscotti into ½-inch (1.25-centimeter) slices and place the cookies on their sides on the cookie sheet.
12. Bake the biscotti for 5 minutes, flip to the other side and cook for 5 more minutes or until lightly browned.

Zucchini and Tomato Frittata

50 minutes

12 servings

Ingredients

1 tablespoon (15 milliliters) plus ½ teaspoon (2.5 milliliters) extra-virgin olive oil, divided

1 cup (240 milliliters) onion, diced small

2 ¼ cups (540 milliliters) medium zucchini, cut into ¼-inch (0.6-centimeter) half-moons

½ cup (120 milliliters) cherry tomatoes, halved

12 large eggs

1 ½ teaspoon (7.5 milliliters) kosher salt

¼ teaspoon (1.2 milliliters) black pepper

2 tablespoons (30 milliliters) fresh basil, chopped

⅓ cup (80 milliliters) Parmesan cheese, grated and divided

Directions

1. Preheat the oven to 350°F (180°C). Grease only the bottom (not the sides) of a 9 x 13-inch (23 x 33-centimeter) pan with oil. Set aside.
2. In a large nonstick skillet, over medium heat, add 1 tablespoon (15 milliliters) olive oil and the onion. Cook for about 5 minutes, stirring occasionally until softened.
3. Add the zucchini and cook for another 6 to 8 minutes on medium-high heat, stirring often. Transfer to a bowl and set aside.
4. Add the cherry tomatoes and the remaining ½ teaspoon (2.5 milliliters) olive oil to the empty pan. Cook over medium-high heat for 3 to 5 minutes until the tomatoes blister and char. Remove from the heat and let cool for 5 minutes.

5. In a large mixing bowl, add the eggs, salt and pepper. Whisk until combined and the egg yolks and whites. Don't overmix.
6. Mix in most of the zucchini mixture (leaving some aside for garnish), basil, and half of the Parmesan to the beaten eggs.
7. Pour egg mixture into the prepared pan, even out the mixture, and sprinkle the top with the remaining Parmesan.
8. Decorate the top with the cooked tomatoes and remaining zucchini slices. Make sure the sautéed tomatoes are facing upwards so you can see the inside of the tomatoes.
9. Bake on the center rack of the oven for 21 to 23 minutes, or until the top is speckled with light golden brown and most of the top is firm. It is ok if the very center of the frittata has the tiniest bit of jiggle, since it will continue to cook as it cools.
10. Run a knife around the edges to loosen the frittata from the pan. Allow to cool for 5 minutes before slicing and serving. Serve warm or at room temperature.

Lemon Ricotta Muffins

32 minutes

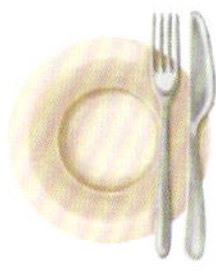
12 muffins

Ingredients

2 cups (480 milliliters) all-purpose flour

1 teaspoon (5 milliliters) baking powder

½ teaspoon (2.5 milliliters) baking soda

½ teaspoon (2.5 milliliters) salt

1 cup (240 milliliters) granulated sugar

1 cup (240 milliliters) ricotta cheese, drained

½ cup (120 milliliters) unsalted butter, softened

1 large egg

1 large lemon, zested and juiced

Lemon Glaze

½ cup (120 milliliters) powdered sugar

2 to 3 (5 to 10 milliliters) teaspoons lemon juice (could also use milk)

In a small bowl, whisk together the powdered sugar and lemon juice (or milk). Pour the glaze over the cooled muffins.

Directions

1. Preheat the oven to 350°F (180°C). Line a 12-cup muffin tin with liners or spray with cooking spray; set aside.
2. In a medium bowl, whisk together the flour, baking powder, baking soda, and salt; set aside.
3. In a separate bowl, combine the granulated sugar, ricotta cheese, and butter. Mix the ingredients until light, about 2 minutes. Add the lemon zest and juice. Pour in the dry ingredients and mix until just combined.
4. Use a muffin scoop to divide the batter equally into 12 cups. Bake for about 21 to 24 minutes, or until a toothpick inserted in the middle of the muffin comes out clean. Let cool on a cooling rack.

Breakfast Bruschetta

15 minutes

4 servings

Ingredients

2 eggs

½ teaspoon (2.5 milliliters) garlic powder

1 tablespoon (milliliters) butter

4 slices ½-inch (1.25-centimeter) thick Italian bread, toasted

5 tablespoons (75 milliliters) garlic and herb or herb-flavored goat cheese

4 to 5 sun-dried tomatoes, chopped

4 to 5 basil leaves, chopped

Olive oil, to drizzle

¼ teaspoon (1.2 milliliters) salt

¼ teaspoon (1.2 milliliters) pepper

TIP

Replace goat cheese with 1 1/2 teaspoons (7.5 milliliters) softened cream cheese.

Directions

1. In a small bowl, scramble eggs well with a whisk or fork.
2. Add the garlic powder to the eggs and mix well.
3. In a small frying pan, add a teaspoon of butter over low heat and swirl it around until the butter coats the pan's surface.
4. Gently pour the eggs into the pan, stirring slowly to break up the egg mixture.
5. Keep stirring the eggs with your spatula over low heat for three more minutes.
6. Once the eggs appear to have silky, slightly shiny curds, remove them from the pan.

To assemble the bruschetta

1. Take 4 slices of toasted Italian bread and spread a generous amount of the softened garlic and herb goat cheese on each slice.
2. Pile a good amount of your soft scrambled eggs on top of the bread.
3. Sprinkle the chopped sun-dried tomatoes and chopped fresh basil on each bruschetta.
4. Drizzle with olive oil and sprinkle with salt & pepper.

Torta Pasqualina (Spinach and Ricotta Pie)

1 hour 50 minutes

4 servings

Ingredients

2 cups (480 milliliters) baby spinach leaves, rinsed and stems removed

1 ½ cups (360 milliliters) ricotta cheese, drained

¼ cup (60 milliliters) pecorino Romano cheese, grated

7 eggs

1 teaspoon (5 milliliters) salt

¼ teaspoon (1.2 milliliters) nutmeg, ground

¼ teaspoon (1.2 milliliters) black pepper

2 sheets (approximately 10-inch (25-centimeter) square) store-bought frozen puff pastry

Olive oil for greasing the pan

TIP

This is a traditional savory pie served around Easter time.

Directions

1. Preheat a large frying pan or a large saucepan over medium heat.
2. Add the spinach to the pan and cook for 2 to 3 minutes, stirring occasionally, until wilted. You may need to do this in batches. Remove the spinach from the heat and let it cool.
3. Once the spinach has cooled, use your hands to squeeze out any excess moisture.
4. Place the spinach onto a cutting board and chop finely.
5. In a large mixing bowl, combine the spinach, ricotta cheese, pecorino Romano cheese, 2 eggs, nutmeg, salt, and pepper. Mix well until all ingredients are thoroughly combined.
6. Preheat oven to 400°F (200°C) and grease an 8-inch (20-centimeter) springform pan with olive oil.
7. Follow the directions to thaw the frozen puff pastry sheets and keep them chilled.
8. Trace a circle on one pastry sheet using the springform pan. This will be the top crust.
9. Place the second sheet of pastry on a lightly floured surface and press the remaining pastry to extend the dough to be large enough to line the springform pan. Line the oiled pan with the extended puff pastry sheet. Cut off excess pastry and use it to patch up where needed.
10. Fill the pastry-lined pan with the spinach-ricotta mixture, and smooth with a spatula to even the surface.
11. Make five deep indentations in the filling using the back of a tablespoon. Carefully crack an egg into each indentation, being careful not to break the yolk. Add a tiny sprinkle of salt to each egg.
12. Use the previously cut circle of pastry to cover the filling, trimming off any excess pastry. Fold the sides onto the top and press the pastry edges together to seal. Brush the top of the pastry with olive oil.
13. Using a sharp knife with an adult, create small vents on the top of the pastry. Bake for 35 to 40 minutes or until the pastry is golden brown and puffed and the filling is firm.
14. Remove the pan from the oven and let the pie cool for at least 30 minutes before releasing it from the springform pan. Serve warm or at room temperature.

Panna Cotta

4 hours and 20 minutes

5 servings

Ingredients

1 cup (240 milliliters) whole milk

2 ½ teaspoons (12.5 milliliters) unflavored gelatin (1 packet Knox gelatin)

2 cups (480 milliliters) heavy whipping cream

½ cup + 1 tablespoon (135 millilters) granulated sugar

1 teaspoon (5 milliliters) vanilla extract

¼ teaspoon (1.2 milliliters) salt

1 cup (240 milliliters) sour cream

Berry Sauce

1 cup (240 milliliters) raspberries, sliced

1 cup (240 milliliters) strawberries, quartered

¼ cup (60 milliliters) granulated sugar

½ tablespoon (7.5 milliliters) lemon juice

In a small saucepan, combine berries, lemon juice, and sugar; remove from heat. When the syrup is at room temperature or barely warm, spoon it over chilled Panna Cotta.

Directions

1. Pour the milk into a medium saucepan and sprinkle the top with gelatin. Let stand for 3 to 5 minutes or until gelatin is softened. Place pan over medium-low heat and stir until gelatin dissolves and mixture is steaming, about 4 to 5 minutes (do not boil).
2. Add heavy whipping cream, sugar, and vanilla. Continue stirring for about 5 minutes, until the sugar is fully dissolved and the mixture is steaming (do not boil). Remove from heat and let cool for 5 minutes.
3. Place sour cream in a medium bowl with a pouring lip. Whisking constantly, gradually add warm cream. Once the mixture is entirely smooth, divide it into 6 glass cups or 8 ramekins. Refrigerate until fully set, 4 to 6 hours.

Small Plates, Sides & Snacks

Antipasto Skewers

30 minutes

20 skewers

Ingredients

20 cheese tortellini

½ cup (120 milliliters) Italian dressing

1 cup (240 milliliters) black olives (20 pieces)

½ cup (120 milliliters) fresh basil leaves

20 slices salami

20 grape tomatoes

1 jar marinated artichoke hearts (20 pieces)

20 slices pepperoni

20 1-inch (2.5-centimeter) mozzarella balls

20 6-inch (15-centimeter) wooden skewers

Directions

1. In a medium pot, cook tortellini according to package directions. Drain and rinse under cold water to stop the cooking process. Transfer to a bowl and toss with Italian dressing. Cover the bowl with plastic wrap and refrigerate for 15 minutes up to 2 hours.
2. Thread the olives, basil, tortellini, salami, tomatoes, artichoke hearts, pepperoni, and cheese onto the wooden skewers, alternating among different colors and textures.
3. Serve with olive oil and balsamic vinegar, with a drizzle of balsamic glaze, or with pesto, if desired.

Caprese Salad

25 minutes

6 servings

Ingredients

1½ pounds (680 grams) ripe tomatoes (3-4 medium) sliced ¼ inch (0.6 centimeters) thick

1 ½ to 2 cups (360 to 480 milliliters) fresh mozzarella sliced ¼ inch (0.6 centimeters) thick

⅓ cup (80 milliliters) fresh basil leaves

3 tablespoons (45 milliliters) olive oil for drizzling

¼ teaspoon (1.2 milliliters) salt

¼ teaspoon (1.2 milliliters) freshly cracked black pepper

2 tablespoons (30 milliliters) balsamic glaze

Directions

1. On a flat serving platter, alternate layering tomato, cheese, and basil leaf.
2. Season generously with salt and pepper, drizzle with extra-virgin olive oil, and drizzle with 2 tablespoons (30 milliliters) of balsamic glaze.

TIP

Top it off with avocado slices to add a creamy texture and delicious flavor to the salad.

Balsamic Bruschetta

20 minutes

8 servings

Ingredients

1 loaf French bread, cut into ¼-inch (0.6-centimeter) slices

1 tablespoon + 2 teaspoons (15 milliliters + 10 milliliters) extra-virgin olive oil

8 Roma (plum) tomatoes, diced

⅓ cup (80 milliliters) fresh basil, chopped

2 tablespoons (30 milliliters) Parmesan cheese, freshly grated

2 garlic cloves, minced

1 tablespoon (15 milliliters) balsamic vinegar

¼ teaspoon (1.2 milliliters) kosher salt

¼ teaspoon (1.2 milliliters) black pepper

Directions

1. Preheat oven to 400°F (200°C).
2. Lightly brush bread slices on both sides with 1 tablespoon (15 milliliters) oil and place on a large baking sheet. Toast bread until golden, 5 to 10 minutes, turning halfway through.
3. Meanwhile, toss tomatoes, basil, parmesan cheese, and garlic in a bowl.
4. Mix in balsamic vinegar, 2 teaspoons (10 milliliters) olive oil, kosher salt, and pepper.
5. Spoon tomato mixture onto toasted bread slices.
6. Serve immediately.

Big Night Salad

15 minutes

6 servings

Ingredients

Vinaigrette

1 cup (240 milliliters) fresh Italian parsley leaves

1 cup (240 milliliters) fresh basil leaves

¼ teaspoon (1.2 milliliters) oregano, dried

2 garlic cloves, peeled

⅓ cup (80 milliliters) red wine vinegar

¾ cup (175 milliliters) extra-virgin olive oil

¾ teaspoon (3.6 milliliters) salt

¼ teaspoon (1.2 milliliters) black pepper

2 teaspoons (10 milliliters) honey

Salad

1 large head romaine lettuce, torn into large, bite-sized pieces

1 large red bell pepper, chopped

1 cup (240 milliliters) cucumbers, seeded and chopped

1 to 2 carrots, peeled into ribbons

20 grape tomatoes, halved

Handful pitted olives

Ricotta salata or feta cheese, crumbled to taste

Directions

1. In a food processor, combine parsley, basil, oregano, garlic, vinegar, oil, salt, pepper and honey and blend.
2. In a large bowl, add lettuce, pepper, cucumber, carrots, tomato, and olives. Right before serving, add about half of the dressing and toss well. Add more dressing as necessary and toss in the cheese, then taste and adjust the seasoning with salt and pepper, if necessary.

Mozzarella Stuffed Arancini (Italian Rice Balls)

1 hour 50 minutes

8 rice balls

Ingredients

Vegetable oil for frying

2 cups (480 milliliters) cooked white rice, cooled

¾ cup (175 milliliters) grated Parmesan cheese, divided

4 eggs, beaten

3 tablespoons (45 milliliters) parsley, minced and divided

6 ounces (170 grams) mozzarella cheese, cut into 8 cubes

1 ½ cups (360 milliliters) Italian-style seasoned breadcrumbs

1 teaspoon (5 milliliters) garlic powder

Marinara sauce for dipping

TIP

Keep your arancini in the fridge until the oil is hot. This will help them hold their shape when added to the hot oil.

Directions

1. Add a few inches of vegetable oil to a heavy pot; heat over medium heat until it reaches 375°F (190°C).
2. In a medium bowl, mix cooked rice, ½ cup (120 milliliters) Parmesan cheese, one beaten egg, 2 tablespoons (30 milliliters) parsley, salt, and pepper.
3. To make the arancini, wet your hands, take a large spoonful of the mixture, put mozzarella on it, then press another spoonful on top and form a ball. Repeat to make all 8 arancini.
4. Make a breading station with the three beaten eggs in one bowl and breadcrumbs in another.
5. Dip each arancino first in the egg and then in the breadcrumbs, shaking off any excess.
6. An adult should complete this step. Once the oil reaches 375°F (190°C), add a couple of arancini and fry until golden brown and cooked throughout (30 seconds to 1 minute).
7. Remove to a paper towel-lined plate to drain, then fry the remaining arancini.
8. Serve the arancini with warm marinara sauce, garnished with remaining Parmesan cheese and chopped parsley.

Italian Wedding Soup

45 minutes

4 servings

Ingredients

1 slice of white bread, torn into pieces
1 clove garlic
¼ medium onion
¼ teaspoon (1.2 milliliters) kosher salt
¼ teaspoon (1.2 milliliters) freshly ground black pepper
¼ cup (60 milliliters) fresh flat-leaf parsley leaves
1 large egg
8 ounces (224 grams) ground beef
8 ounces (224 grams) ground pork
3 tablespoons (45 milliliters) grated Parmesan cheese
3 tablespoons (45 milliliters) olive oil
1 medium carrot, chopped
1 celery rib, chopped
¾ medium onion, chopped
6 cups (1,440 milliliters) chicken broth
1 Parmesan rind, optional
¼ teaspoon kosher salt
¼ teaspoon freshly ground black pepper
½ cup (120 milliliters) couscous
4 cups (960 milliliters) escarole, chopped
2 tablespoons (30 milliliters) chopped fresh parsley
Extra-virgin olive oil for serving

Directions

1. Line a rimmed baking sheet with parchment or foil.
2. In a food processor, place the bread, garlic, onion, ½ teaspoon (2.5 milliliters) salt, and a few grinds of black pepper; pulse until very finely ground. Add the parsley and pulse until finely chopped. Add the egg and pulse until combined. Add the beef, pork, and Parmesan; pulse until very well mixed. Transfer the mixture to a bowl. Roll the mixture into 1-inch (2.5-centimeter) meatballs, transferring them to the prepared baking sheet.
3. For the soup: Heat the olive oil in a dutch oven or large, wide pot over medium-high heat. Add half of the meatballs and cook, gently stirring occasionally, until browned on most sides and just cooked through, about 3 to 4 minutes. Remove the meatballs to the baking sheet; repeat with the remaining meatballs.
4. Add the carrot, celery, and onion to the pot and cook, stirring occasionally, until starting to soften, about 5 minutes. Add the chicken broth, Parmesan rind if using, ½ teaspoon (2.5 milliliters) salt, and a few grinds of black pepper; bring to a brisk simmer. Add the pasta or couscous and cook according to the package directions for al dente.
5. Add the escarole and meatballs to the soup and return to a simmer. Simmer until the escarole is slightly wilted, about 2 minutes. Remove the Parmesan rind and discard. Sprinkle with the parsley and top with a drizzle of extra-virgin olive oil. Serve with more Parmesan on the side.

Roasted Vegetables

40 minutes

8 servings

Ingredients

2 medium zucchini, sliced in half lengthwise and then into half-moons

2 medium yellow squash, sliced in half lengthwise and then into half-moons

2 bell peppers (red, yellow, or orange), cut into thick strips and then cut in half

16 ounces (455 grams) baby Bella mushrooms, sliced in half lengthwise

1 medium red onion, cut into large chunks

3 garlic cloves, minced

⅓ cup (80 milliliters) extra-virgin olive oil

2 teaspoons (10 milliliters) Italian seasoning

½ teaspoon (2.5 milliliters) kosher salt (plus more to taste)

¼ teaspoon (1.2 milliliters) pepper

Italian parsley to garnish, diced (optional)

Directions

1. Preheat oven to 425°F (220°C) and line two baking sheets with parchment paper; set aside.
2. Place the zucchini, squash, peppers, mushrooms, onions, and garlic in a large mixing bowl. Pour on the olive oil, herb seasoning, kosher salt, and pepper. Toss well to combine. Divide the veggies between the two baking sheets.
3. Bake in the top half of the oven, rotating pans halfway through. Serve with diced fresh parsley.

TIP

Make your own Italian seasoning by combining 1 tablespoon each dried oregano, basil, rosemary, and thyme.

Potato Croquettes

1 hour 50 minutes

20 servings

Ingredients

1½ pounds (681 grams) of potatoes, riced or mashed

1 egg lightly beaten, room temperature

½ cup (120 milliliters) pecorino Romano cheese, grated

1 tablespoon (15 milliliters) parsley, finely chopped

¼ teaspoon (1.2 milliliters) salt

¼ teaspoon (1.2 milliliters) pepper

¼ cup (60 milliliters) flour

2 eggs slightly beaten, room temperature

1 tablespoon (15 milliliters) water

¾ cup (175 milliliters) breadcrumbs

6 teaspoons (30 milliliters) olive oil

Directions

1. Combine potatoes with the beaten egg, Romano cheese, parsley, salt and pepper.
2. Divide the mixture into 20 croquettes.
3. Prepare 3 shallow bowls with flour in the first, 2 beaten eggs with 1 tablespoon (15 milliliters) water for an egg wash in the second, and breadcrumbs in the third.
4. Roll each croquette, one by one, in the flour, removing any excess.
5. Dip each floured croquette in the egg wash and roll in the breadcrumbs.
6. With an adult, in batches of 5 croquettes, "pan fry" in 1 to 1½ teaspoons (5 to 7.5 milliliters) of olive oil.
7. Once all the croquettes have been pan-fried, place them in a baking dish and bake them in a preheated oven at 375°F (190°C) for 15 minutes.
8. Serve immediately.

Entrées

Chicken "Marsala"

 30 minutes

 2 to 4 servings

Ingredients

1 pound (454 grams) chicken breasts, boneless and skinless

¼ teaspoon (1.2 milliliters) salt

¼ teaspoon (1.2 milliliters) pepper

2 tablespoons (30 milliliters) olive oil

½ cup (120 milliliters) all-purpose flour

2 tablespoons (30 milliliters) butter, unsalted

1 shallot, peeled and chopped

2 garlic cloves, peeled and chopped

2 cups (480 milliliters) cremini mushrooms, thinly sliced

1 ½ cups (360 milliliters) chicken or vegetable broth

¼ cup (60 milliliters) heavy cream

1 tablespoon white vinegar (15 milliliters)

½ teaspoon (2.5 milliliters) ground mustard powder

1 teaspoon (5 milliliters) thyme, dried

1 tablespoon (15 milliliters) fresh parsley, finely chopped (for garnish)

TIP

This kid-friendly recipe does not contain Marsala wine, and if you don't have ground mustard powder, replace it with 1 teaspoon (5 milliliters) Dijon mustard.

Directions

1. Carefully slice each chicken breast in half lengthwise (horizontally) and place one at a time between 2 sheets of cling wrap. Carefully flatten the chicken breasts with a rolling pin until they are approximately ¼ inch (0.6 centimeters) thick. All should have a uniform thickness.
2. Season both sides of each chicken breast with salt and pepper. Prepare a shallow plate with flour (save 1 tablespoon (15 milliliters) for later) and dip the chicken into the flour, evenly coating on both sides. Set aside.
3. Carefully heat oil in a large skillet over medium-high for 2 minutes until it sizzles. Add the chicken and fry for about 4 minutes per side until golden brown and fully cooked. The internal temperature of the chicken should reach 165°F (75°C). Transfer the chicken to a plate.
4. In the same skillet with the chicken drippings, melt butter and sauté mushrooms until golden brown on both sides, about 5 minutes. Add a little more olive oil if needed.
5. Add shallots and garlic to the mushrooms, scraping up bits from the bottom. Mix in 1 tablespoon (15 milliliters) flour. Pour in broth and vinegar and simmer over medium heat for about 5 to 7 minutes, until reduced by half and thickened.
6. Add the heavy cream, mustard and thyme. Return the chicken to the sauce mixture and simmer another 2 to 3 minutes to thicken.
7. Garnish with parsley and serve immediately with pasta, rice, or over mashed potatoes.

DEFINITION

Sear: A cooking technique that involves quickly cooking the surface of food at a high temperature to create a brown crust.

Caprese Pizza

1 hour 30 minutes

2 to 4 servings

Ingredients

1 ½ cup (360 milliliters) plus 2 tablespoons (30 milliliters) all-purpose flour

½ teaspoon (2.5 milliliters) instant yeast

½ teaspoon (2.5 milliliters) fine salt

¾ cup (175 millimeters) lukewarm water

⅔ tablespoons (10 milliliters) olive oil

3 to 4 medium tomatoes, sliced

5 ounces (142 grams) fresh mozzarella

⅓ cup (80 milliliters) tomato sauce – see recipe at right

Fresh basil, chopped

¼ teaspoon (1.2 milliliters) fine salt

Extra-virgin olive oil for drizzling

Pizza Sauce
3 minutes
Makes 2 ½ cups (600 milliliters), enough for one pizza

1 20-ounce (567 gram) can of Italian plum tomatoes
¼ teaspoon (1.2 milliliters) salt
¼ cup (60 milliliters) olive oil

1. In a large bowl, smash the tomatoes with your clean hands until they become a chunky sauce.
2. Add salt and olive oil and stir.

TIP
Add toppings of your choice.

Directions

1. In a large bowl, mix flour, yeast, and salt. Add water and olive oil and stir to combine. If the dough is lumpy, add another 1 tablespoon (15 milliliters) of water to ensure all the flour is well combined.
2. Cover the bowl with a damp towel and let rest in a warm place until it has doubled in size.
3. When the dough is ready, preheat the oven to 450°F (230°C) with a rack in the lowest position.
4. If you have a pizza stone, use it, or cut parchment paper and place it on a large baking sheet.
5. Using a spatula, scrape the sides of the bowl and pour the dough onto the stone. Sprinkle with flour and gently press the dough out with your fingers from the center, forming a large round pizza.
6. Spread the pizza sauce on top of the dough, top with tomato slices and mozzarella, and sprinkle with salt.
7. Bake pizza in the oven for 15 to 20 minutes.
8. Remove pizza from the oven. Sprinkle with basil and drizzle with olive oil.

Meatballs

45 minutes

8 servings

Ingredients

2 cups (480 milliliters) breadcrumbs

1 cup (240 milliliters) milk

2 cups (480 milliliters) white onions, finely chopped

4 tablespoons (60 milliliters) canola oil

2 tablespoons (30 milliliters) salt

1½ tablespoons (22.5 milliliters) finely ground black pepper

5 pounds (2.25 grams) ground beef

4 eggs, whole or whisked

1 cup (240 milliliters) provolone cheese, diced small

1 cup (240 milliliters) mozzarella cheese, diced small

1 cup (240 milliliters) Parmesan cheese, finely grated

Directions

1. In a bowl, soak breadcrumbs in milk for at least an hour until very soft.
2. In a skillet, cook onions in canola oil on medium-low heat until translucent and very tender. Strain any excess oil, then season with salt and pepper.
3. In a large mixing bowl, add ground beef, milk, and breadcrumb mixture, which should be a soft, cohesive mass. Add egg, provolone, mozzarella, and Parmesan cheese.
4. Mix well for 10 to 15 minutes, then refrigerate the meatball mixture for about an hour.
5. Preheat oven to 450°F (230°C). Scoop or hand roll portions into the size you want for meatballs.
6. Place meatballs on a baking sheet and bake for 5 minutes on each side, rotating occasionally to get color on all sides.

Homemade Pasta

55 minutes

6 servings

Ingredients

2 cups (480 milliliters) breadcrumbs

2 cups (480 milliliters) all-purpose flour

3 large eggs

½ teaspoon (2.5 milliliters) sea salt

½ tablespoon (7.5 milliliters) extra-virgin olive oil

TIP

For this recipe, you do not need a pasta maker; you only need a sharp knife to cut the dough into strips. Other easy pasta to make with a rolling pin and knife are fettucine, farfalle, and gnocchi.

Directions

1. Place flour in a pile on a flat surface and make a well in the center of it.
2. Once the well is formed, add the eggs, salt, and olive oil to it.
3. With a fork, gently stir the flour into the eggs and other ingredients until combined.
4. Knead everything together with clean hands. Take your time and bring it all together until a cohesive mass is formed. When you press your thumb into the dough, it should bounce back a little bit.
5. Place a damp towel over the dough and allow it to rest for about an hour.
6. When the dough has finished resting, shape it into a fat log and cut it into 5 or 6 equal sections.
7. Flour your workspace well and roll the dough into a long strip using your rolling pin. With each pass, as you roll, lift the dough, re-dust the counter beneath, and flip it over. You should have a long, thin piece of dough when finished. It should be just about paper-thin but strong enough to be lifted off the countertop.
8. Dust the strip of dough with more flour. Starting with the short end, loosely fold like an accordion.
9. Carefully use a sharp knife to cut the stack across the folds into thin strips. You can cut the strips as thin or thick as you prefer (like thin linguini or wide pappardelle), keeping the width consistent.
10. Unroll the bundle of noodles and lay them across a flat surface or the back of a chair. Let them dry for about 15 minutes.
11. Continue rolling out and cutting the pasta until you've worked through all the dough.
12. Bring a pot of salted water to a boil. Add the fresh pasta and cook for 4 to 5 minutes, until chewy and al dente (taste one of the noodles to check). Serve with your favorite sauce.

Chicken Parmesan

45 minutes

6 servings

Ingredients

1 pound (454 grams) chicken breasts, thinly sliced

¼ teaspoon (1.2 milliliters) salt

¼ teaspoon (1.2 milliliters) pepper

¼ cup (60 milliliters) all-purpose flour

2 eggs

1 cup (240 milliliters) panko breadcrumbs

¾ cup (175 milliliters) Parmesan cheese, grated

¾ cup (175 milliliters) marinara sauce

¾ cup (175 milliliters) mozzarella cheese, shredded

1 tablespoon (15 milliliters) Italian seasoning (optional)

TIP

For a vegetarian option, use sliced eggplant instead of chicken.

Directions

1. Preheat the oven to 450°F (230°C).
2. Pat the chicken breasts dry and season with salt and pepper.
3. Dip each piece of chicken in the flour, shake off the excess, and set aside.
4. In a shallow bowl, whisk together the eggs until smooth. In a separate bowl, mix the breadcrumbs and ½ cup (120 milliliters) Parmesan cheese until combined (reserve the other ¼ cup (60 milliliters) of Parmesan cheese to sprinkle on top).
5. Dip each floured piece of chicken breast into the egg mixture and shake off any excess. Immediately dip the egg-coated chicken into the breadcrumb/cheese mixture, making sure to firmly pat the breadcrumbs into the chicken so they stick. Repeat with all 6 pieces and set them aside. Let the chicken sit and rest for 10 minutes.
6. Heat a pan with oil on medium heat. Once the oil is hot, add the chicken and pan-fry chicken pieces for a few minutes per side.
7. Once each side is golden brown, transfer the chicken pieces to a pan and layer each with 2 tablespoons (30 milliliters) of marinara sauce, 2 tablespoons (30 milliliters) of mozzarella cheese, and two teaspoons (10 milliliters) of grated Parmesan cheese. If you'd like, sprinkle a little Italian seasoning on top.
8. Bake the breasts for 8 to 10 minutes or until the cheese is fully melted and bubbly.

Simple Sauces

Pesto

15 minutes

1 ½ cups (360 milliliters)

Ingredients

2 tablespoons (30 milliliters) pine nuts

3 cups (720 milliliters) basil leaves

2 garlic cloves, smashed

½ cup (120 milliliters) freshly grated Parmigiano-Reggiano cheese

½ cup (120 milliliters extra-virgin olive oil

1 teaspoon (5 milliliters) kosher salt

Directions

1. In a small skillet over medium heat, toast pine nuts, stirring frequently, until golden, about 5 minutes. Transfer nuts to the bowl of a food processor to cool.
2. Pulse nuts with basil, garlic, and cheese until blended, scraping down the sides of the bowl as needed, 5 pulses. With the machine running, slowly pour in olive oil and purée until almost smooth. Season with salt.

Alfredo Sauce

10 minutes

2 cups (480 milliliters)

Ingredients

½ cup (120 milliliters) butter

1 ½ cups (360 milliliters) heavy whipping cream

2 teaspoons (10 milliliters) garlic, minced

½ teaspoon (2.5 milliliters) Italian seasoning

½ teaspoon (2.5 milliliters) salt

¼ teaspoon (1.2 milliliters) pepper

2 cups (480 milliliters) Parmesan cheese, freshly grated

Directions

1. In a large skillet, add the butter and cream and simmer over low heat for 2 minutes.
2. Whisk in the garlic, Italian seasoning, salt, and pepper for one minute.
3. Whisk in the Parmesan cheese until melted.
4. Serve immediately.

Orecchiette with Broccoli Rabe and Sausage

30 minutes

6 servings

Ingredients

Olive oil for cooking

¼ cup (60 milliliters) onion, minced

¼ cup (60 milliliters) fennel, minced

2 tablespoons (30 milliliters) fennel seeds, toasted well

1 cup (240 milliliters) white vinegar

1 cup (240 milliliters) water

3 pounds (1,36 grams) Italian pork sausage, ground

1 ¼ cups (300 milliliters) garlic, chopped

¼ teaspoon salt

¼ teaspoon pepper

8 cups (1,920 milliliters) marinara sauce

1 cup (240 milliliters) basil

2 bunches broccoli rabe, chopped and blanched

2 pounds (908 grams) dry orecchiette pasta (or any dry pasta)

1 tablespoon butter (optional for finishing)

Directions

1. In a medium-sized pot, warm oil, then add onion, fennel, and fennel seeds, cooking until tender—about 10 minutes or until all ingredients are translucent but not browned. Add vinegar and water and reduce by half.
2. Add pork sausage and garlic and cook until the pork has gone from pink to white. Add salt and pepper to taste, then add marinara sauce and simmer for about an hour. Finish with basil, broccoli rabe, and chili flakes.
3. Cook pasta in a pot of boiling salted water until al dente, strain, and toss with butter if desired.
4. Taste the sauce for seasoning, then serve it with the pasta.

Lasagna

1 hour 20 minutes

12 slices

Ingredients

1 pound (454 grams) ground beef (15 to 20% fat content)

1 medium onion, finely diced

3 garlic cloves, minced

4 tablespoons (60 milliliters) extra virgin olive oil

3 cups (720 milliliters) marinara sauce

½ teaspoon (2.5 milliliters) sea salt

¼ teaspoon (1.2 milliliters) black pepper, freshly ground

¼ teaspoon (1.2 milliliters) dried thyme

½ teaspoon (2.5 milliliters) granulated sugar

2 tablespoons (30 milliliters) parsley, finely chopped

9 lasagna noodles, cooked al dente

3 cups (720 milliliters) ricotta cheese

1 large egg

3 tablespoons (90 milliliters) parsley, finely chopped, plus more to garnish

4 cups (1,200 milliliters) mozzarella cheese, shredded, divided

Directions

1. Place a deep pan or dutch oven over medium-high heat and add oil, ground beef, and diced onion. Sauté, breaking up the meat for 5 minutes or until the beef is no longer pink. Add garlic and sauté another minute until fragrant.

2. Add broth and stir for 2 minutes. Add marinara, salt, pepper, thyme, sugar, and 2 tablespoons parsley. Bring to a simmer, then cover and cook for 5 minutes.
3. In a large mixing bowl, combine ricotta, 1 cup (240 milliliters) mozzarella, egg, and remaining parsley. Mix well.
4. Preheat the oven to 375°F (190°C). Bring a large pot of water to a boil, then add salt and lasagna noodles. Cook until al dente, according to the package directions.
5. Spread ½ cup (120 milliliters) meat sauce in the bottom of a deep 9 x 13-inch (23 x 33-centimeter) casserole dish. Add 3 noodles, spread on ⅓ of the meat sauce, and sprinkle with 1 cup (240 milliliters) mozzarella cheese. Spoon on and spread the top with ½ of the ricotta cheese sauce.
6. Repeat step 5 until you have 3 layers of noodles.
7. Poke 9 to 12 toothpicks into the surface of your lasagna (to keep the foil from sticking to the cheese). Cover with foil and bake at 375°F (190°C) for 45 minutes. Remove the foil and broil for 3 to 5 minutes or until the cheese turns golden. Let the lasagna rest for 30 minutes before slicing.

Pasta with Tomato Sauce allo Scarpariello

25 minutes

4 servings

Ingredients

5 cups water

¼ teaspoon (1.2 milliliters) salt

⅓ cup (80 milliliters) extra-virgin olive oil

1 clove garlic, peeled

Basil, a handful, washed and torn into pieces

1 cup (240 milliliters) cherry tomatoes, cut in half

2 cups (480 milliliters) tomato purée

¼ teaspoon (1.2 milliliters) pepper

1 ½ cups (355 milliliters) penne or spaghetti (see homemade pasta recipe page 50)

¼ cup (60 milliliters) Parmigiano Reggiano cheese, grated

Directions

1. Bring a large pot of salted water to a boil.
2. In a large frying pan, heat the olive oil; sauté garlic until it softens, then add some basil.
3. Add the tomatoes; when they have softened, pour in the tomato purée.
4. Simmer for approximately 15 minutes; remove the garlic and add salt and pepper.

5. Add pasta to the pot of boiling water and cook al dente. Drain, then add pasta to the saucepan. Cook for 2 to 3 more minutes, until the pasta is cooked.
6. Lower the heat, add the cheese, and combine with sauce and pasta. The cheese should melt completely.
7. Serve immediately with fresh basil and extra cheese.

DEFINITION

Al dente: Italian term which translates to "to the tooth." Used to describe the consistency of vegetables, beans, rice, or pasta cooked to be firm when bitten.

Ricotta Gnocchi

25 minutes

4 to 6 servings

Ingredients

6 cups (1,440 milliliters) ricotta cheese

4 cups (960 milliliters) Parmesan cheese, grated

3 eggs

4 ½ cups (1,080 milliliters) flour, plus 1 cup (240 milliliters) for rolling

1 tablespoon (15 milliliters) black pepper

1 cup (240 milliliters) tomato sauce

Directions

1. In a large bowl, add ricotta cheese, Parmesan cheese, eggs, flour, and pepper. Stir to combine, then refrigerate for at least two hours.
2. Flour a table or countertop and roll the mixture into a log with both hands. Cut the log into 1-inch (2.5-centimeter) pieces. Use the back of a fork to add ridge lines to the individual pieces.
3. In a medium pot, bring salted water to a boil. Add gnocchi to a perforated basket, submerge in the water, and stir. When the gnocchi are floating, they are done.
4. Serve with tomato sauce or sauce of your choice.

Risotto alla Milanese

45 minutes

4 to 6 servings

Ingredients

6 cups (1,200 milliliters) vegetable stock

2 cups (480 milliliters) arborio rice

1½ tablespoons (22.5 milliliters) unsalted butter

1 small yellow onion, finely chopped

1 tablespoon (15 milliliters) extra-virgin olive oil

1 teaspoon (5 milliliters) saffron

⅓ cup (80 milliliters) Parmigiano Reggiano, grated

½ cup (120 milliliters) heavy cream

Directions

1. In a large bowl, combine rice and stock; whisk to release starch. Pour into a mesh strainer over a large bowl and allow to drain, shaking off excess liquid.
2. Melt 1 ½ tablespoons (22.5 milliliters) butter in a large sauté pan over low heat. Add the onion and cook gently to sweat it until soft and translucent, about 5 minutes.
3. Add the rice and toast it over high heat for 1 minute, stirring occasionally until the rice and onion are well coated with butter. Start to add broth in 1 cup (240 milliliter) increments. Let the rice cook away and absorb the liquid before adding more. Stir occasionally. Add the saffron to the second cup and continue cooking the same way. It should take around 16 to 20 minutes, depending on how well done you want the rice. Salt as needed.
4. Remove the saucepan from the heat, then add the remaining butter and cheese. Mix well for a soft, creamy consistency. Cover and let sit for 1 minute, then serve.

Pasta Primavera

30 minutes

4 to 6 servings

Ingredients

2 pounds (908 grams) dry penne pasta

6 tablespoons (90 milliliters) extra-virgin olive oil

3 cloves garlic, minced

8 ounces (224 grams) button mushrooms, quartered

2 cups (480 milliliters) small broccoli florets, blanched

1 cup (240 milliliters) frozen peas

5 small zucchini, quartered lengthwise and cut to 1-inch (2.5-centimeter) lengths, blanched

1 cup (240 milliliters) Parmesan cheese, grated

4 tablespoons (60 milliliters) unsalted butter

Kosher salt and pepper, to taste

2 cups (480 milliliters) cherry tomatoes, cut in half

4 tablespoons (60 milliliters) basil, shredded

Directions

1. Cook pasta in boiling water with a pinch of salt and a dash of olive oil until al dente.
2. Heat 5 tablespoons (75 milliliters) of olive oil in a 12-inch (30.5-centimeter) skillet over medium heat. Add two-thirds of the garlic and cook until golden, about 3 minutes. Add broccoli, peas, zucchini; and cook for 3 more minutes. Add cooked pasta, Parmesan, and butter. Season with salt and pepper and toss to combine.
3. Transfer to a serving dish.
4. Bring remaining olive oil, garlic, tomatoes, and basil to a simmer over medium heat. Pour over pasta.

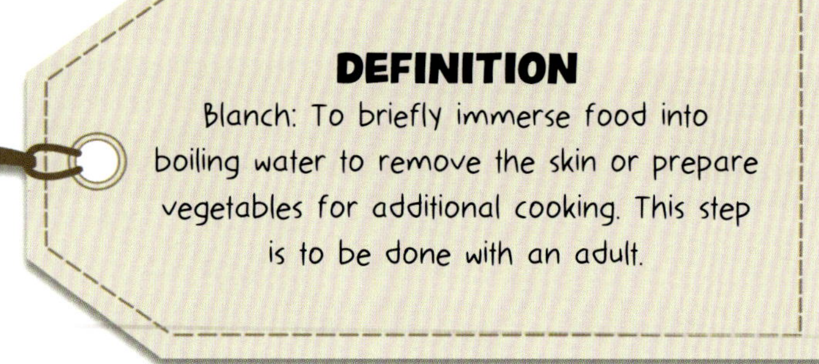

Pasta Bolognese

2 hours 15 minutes

4 to 6 servings

Ingredients

1 medium onion, coarsely chopped

1 large fennel bulb, coarsely chopped

1 large carrot, coarsely chopped

½ cup (120 milliliters) olive oil

1 teaspoon (5 milliliters) crushed red pepper flakes

3 large garlic cloves, finely chopped

1 pound (454 grams) ground chicken

1 pound (454 grams) ground beef

2 cups (480 milliliters) tomato sauce

2 cups (480 milliliters) beef stock

Salt and freshly ground black pepper

¼ cup (60 milliliters) butter

½ cup (120 milliliters) Parmesan cheese

Pinch of red pepper flakes

TIP

Any shape of pasta is great to serve with this sauce.

Directions

1. In a food processor, grind onion, fennel, and carrot until very fine.
2. In a large saucepan, heat olive oil over low heat. Add onion, fennel, carrot, pepper flakes, and garlic; simmer, stirring occasionally, for about 30 minutes or until moisture evaporates.
3. Remove the vegetables from the pan, leaving a little remaining olive oil. Then, add ground chicken and beef to the same pan, stirring frequently. Add tomato sauce and stock to the saucepan when the meat is brown.
4. Return vegetables to pan, stir everything together, and simmer over medium-high heat, stirring occasionally, for 1½ hours or until sauce thickens and is reduced by one quarter. Season to taste with salt and pepper.
5. Serve over your favorite pasta, adding butter, Parmesan, and a pinch of red pepper flakes.

Desserts

Tartufi

3 hours and 15 minutes

7 servings

Ingredients

4 cups (960 milliliters) chocolate ice cream, slightly softened

2 cups (480 milliliters) vanilla ice cream, slightly softened

8 maraschino cherries, stemmed and pitted

1 ½ cups (360 milliliters) crushed chocolate sandwich cookies, plus extra for plating

Directions

1. Line four 2-cup (480 milliliters) domed glass bowls with plastic wrap to extend at least 3 inches (8 centimeters) over all sides. Working one bowl at a time, scoop 1 cup (240 milliliters) of chocolate ice cream into the bowl. Create a crater in the center, pushing the ice cream up the sides of the bowl. Place in the freezer. Repeat this with the 3 remaining bowls, placing them in the freezer as you go. Freeze for 30 minutes.
2. Remove the bowls from the freezer. Working with one bowl at a time, add ½ cup (120 milliliters) vanilla ice cream to the crater. Create another crater in the vanilla ice cream and add 2 cherries. Cover with vanilla ice cream to enclose them. Gather the plastic wrap hanging over the sides of the bowl and wrap it around the ice cream, creating a sphere as best as possible. Place into the freezer as you go and freeze until firm, about 2 hours (and up to 2 to 3 days in a sealed container).
3. Place the crushed cookies on a plate. Remove the plastic wrap from the bowls and roll each ice cream sphere in the cookies to coat thoroughly. (If not serving immediately, return to the freezer.) Spread more cookie crumbs on 8 serving plates. Cut each tartufo vertically and place half a tartufo on each plate. Serve immediately.

TIP

The "sphere" will likely be flat on the bottom. This is fine and will ensure that it sits nicely on the plate.

Zeppole

25 minutes

16 small zeppole

Ingredients

1 cup (240 milliliters) all-purpose flour

1 teaspoon (5 milliliters) baking powder

2 teaspoons (10 milliliters) granulated sugar

½ teaspoon (2.5 milliliters) vanilla extract

½ cup (120 milliliters) water

4 cups (960 milliliters) vegetable oil

½ cup (120 milliliters) confectioners' sugar

Directions

1. In a large bowl, whisk together the flour, baking powder, granulated sugar, vanilla, and water. Whisk until the dough reaches a sticky, even consistency, then roll into small golf-ball-size dough balls. Add more flour if necessary.
2. Under adult supervision, heat 2 cups (480 milliliters) of oil to 375°F (190°C) in a frying pan (or deep fryer).
3. Carefully add dough balls to the heated oil, turning them as needed until golden, about 5 minutes.
4. Transfer to a paper towel-lined plate to drain.
5. Fill a paper bag with confectioners' sugar, seal the bag, and shake to coat the zeppole.

Cioccolata Calda (Italian Hot Chocolate)

17 minutes

4 servings

Ingredients

¼ cup (60 milliliters) unsweetened cocoa powder

2 tablespoons (30 milliliters) cornstarch

2 cups (480 milliliters) whole milk, plus more as needed

¼ cup (60 milliliters) granulated sugar

6 tablespoons (90 milliliters) 70% dark chocolate, chopped

Directions

1. In a medium bowl, whisk together the cocoa powder and cornstarch until well mixed.
2. In a medium saucepan over medium heat, add the milk and the sugar, whisking occasionally, until the sugar has melted and the milk starts to steam (roughly 160°F/71°C), 3 to 4 minutes.
3. Remove the saucepan from the heat and pour some hot milk into the cocoa-cornstarch mixture, whisking until you have a uniform paste. Slowly pour the rest of the milk in, bit by bit, whisking constantly to keep the mixture uniform.
4. Add the chopped chocolate to the bowl, ensure it's submerged, and let it sit until it melts, about 1 minute. Whisk it into the mixture.
5. Return the mixture to the saucepan over medium heat, whisking frequently, until it starts to bubble, about 3 minutes (this will begin to activate the cornstarch). Continue cooking, whisking constantly (especially around the bubbling edges), until the mixture has thickened slightly—the bubbles will suddenly look much bigger and thicker. Turn off the heat, but continue whisking for another minute as the residual heat helps the mixture thicken.
6. Divide the hot chocolate among 4 small mugs.

Pignoli Cookies

34 minutes

40 cookies

Ingredients

1 15-ounce (425 gram) can of almond paste, finely crumbled

1 ½ cups (360 milliliters) confectioners' sugar

2 tablespoons (30 milliliters) honey

¼ teaspoon (1.2 milliliters) ground cinnamon

¼ teaspoon (1.2 milliliters) fine salt

2 large egg whites

1 lemon, zested

½ to ¾ cups (120 to 175 milliliters) pine nuts

Directions

1. Preheat the oven to 350°F (180°C) and line baking sheets with parchment paper or silicone baking mats.
2. In a large bowl, beat the almond paste at high speed until it is really broken up. Add the confectioners' sugar and mix until well combined.
3. Add the honey, cinnamon, salt, egg whites and lemon zest; mix until well combined and very thick, about 5 minutes.
4. Fill a disposable pastry bag with the dough. Push the dough towards the tip and cut the tip off the bag. Pipe 1-inch (2.5-centimeter) balls onto the prepared sheet trays. Top with the pine nuts, pressing them into the dough to secure.
5. Bake until the cookies are golden, 12 to 14 minutes.

Cherry Gelato

4 hours and 30 minutes

6 servings

Ingredients

3 cups (720 milliliters) cherries

1 cup (240 milliliters) milk

7 tablespoons (105 milliliters) sugar, divided

1 tablespoon (15 milliliters) vanilla extract

Zest of 1 lemon

Directions

1. Pit the cherries and cut them into pieces; distribute them on a tray and put them in the freezer for at least 4 hours.
2. Heat the milk with 4 tablespoons (60 milliliters) sugar, vanilla, and lemon zest. Once the milk comes to a boil, carefully pour through cheese cloth into a measuring cup and let it cool. Then, pour the milk into an ice cube tray and place it in the freezer for 4 hours.
3. In a medium bowl blend the cherries, the frozen milk, and 3 tablespoons (45 milliliters) of sugar. Freeze the gelato until ready to serve.

TIP

Once assembled, refrigerate for at least 5 hours or overnight before serving.

Chiacchiere (Crostoli)

1 hour 10 minutes

8 servings

Ingredients

3 cups (720 milliliters) all-purpose flour

1 tablespoon (15 milliliters) baking powder

¼ cup (60 milliliters) sugar

¼ teaspoon (1.2 milliliters) salt

4 tablespoons (60 milliliters) butter, softened

2 eggs

1 lemon and its zest

1 to 2 tablespoons (15 to 30 milliliters) warm water or milk if needed

Vegetable oil for frying

Confectioners' sugar for dusting

Directions

1. In a large mixing bowl, sift flour and baking powder. Add sugar, salt, and softened/melted butter.
2. Add lightly beaten eggs and lemon zest and mix with a fork. Stir in milk.
3. Knead the dough with clean hands until smooth but still firm. Add a tablespoon of water or warm milk if the dough feels too firm and crumbly.
4. Wrap the dough in plastic wrap and rest for at least 30 minutes.

5. You can let it rest overnight in the fridge; make sure to remove it from the refrigerator an hour before starting to work with the dough.
6. Once the dough is "rested," cut off a ½-inch (13-milliliter) piece and sprinkle it with flour.
7. Using a hand roller, roll the dough lightly, fold it in half, and roll a little thinner again.
8. Repeat the folding process, preferably 2 times.
9. Cut the dough into strips 1 inch (2.5 centimeters) or 2 inches (5 centimeters) wide by 4 inches (10 centimeters) long, scored in the center.
10. Have an adult preheat vegetable oil in a deep pan or fryer. The best temperature to start frying the dough is about 350°F (180°C). You can measure it with a kitchen thermometer. If you don't have one, try frying a small piece of the dough; the oil is ready if it bubbles and the dough comes up floating in less than 3 seconds.
11. Once the oil is heated, turn the temperature to medium-low to prevent oil from overheating.
12. Fry crostoli for a few minutes on each side; once they're lightly browned, remove from oil to a paper towel to absorb excess oil.
13. Place fried crostoli on a serving plate and generously dust with confectioners' sugar.

TIP

Instead of hand-rolling the dough, use a pasta machine. The best thickness setting on the pasta machine for ready-to-cut crostoli is 5-6 (1.2 to 1.5 millimeters).

Creamy Ricotta Cheesecake

2 hours and 30 minutes

12 servings

Ingredients

1 cup (240 milliliters) graham cracker crumbs

¼ cup (60 milliliters) all-purpose flour

3 tablespoons (45 milliliters) sugar

¼ cup (60 milliliters) butter, melted

1 pound (454 grams) cream cheese

1 ½ pounds (681 grams) whole-milk ricotta cheese

6 eggs

1 ¼ cups (300 milliliters) sugar

1 tablespoon (15 milliliters) vanilla extract

Directions

1. Preheat the oven to 350°F (180°C). Line the bottom of a 10-inch (25-centimeter) springform pan with waxed paper. Wrap the outside of the pan with aluminum foil.
2. In a medium bowl, mix graham cracker crumbs, flour, sugar, and butter until blended.
3. Press the crumb mixture into the bottom of the pan and press down so the crust evenly covers the bottom.
4. Bake crust for 15 minutes or until golden brown. Remove from oven and reduce heat to 325°F (163°C).

5. In a food processor or blender, purée cream cheese and ricotta until smooth. Transfer to a large mixing bowl, then add eggs, sugar, and vanilla; whisk until blended. Pour mixture into graham cracker crust and place springform pan into a larger pan. Pour water into the larger pan to cover halfway up the sides of the springform pan. Bake for 2 hours. Turn off the oven, open the door, and allow the cheesecake to cool for at least an hour. Remove from oven and refrigerate overnight.
6. When removing the cheesecake from the springform pan, run a hot, wet knife around the edge of the cheesecake before removing the pan's collar. Hold a plate against the top of the pan and carefully flip the cake onto the plate. Serve with fresh berries.

Tiramisu

30 minutes

9 servings

Ingredients

21 lady finger cookies

1 cup (240 milliliters) chocolate milk

1 cup (240 milliliters) mascarpone

1 ¼ cups (300 milliliters) whipping cream

1 ½ tablespoons (22.5 milliliters) powdered sugar

TIP

Once assembled, refrigerate for at least 5 hours or overnight before serving.

Topping

½ cup (120 milliliters) chocolate chips

2 to 3 tablespoons (30 to 45 milliliters) unsweetened cocoa powder

Directions

1. In a medium bowl, add mascarpone, whipping cream, and sugar; whip until thick.
2. In a medium bowl, add the chocolate milk and dunk lady fingers one at a time into the milk to coat.
3. Add the coated lady fingers to the bottom of a 9 x 13-inch (23 x 33 centimeter) baking dish. Each layer should have 7 to 8 cookies. Spread with ½ of the cream mixture.
4. Sprinkle with chocolate flakes and continue with remaining 1 or 2 layers.
5. Sprinkle top layer with chocolate flakes or dust with cocoa powder just prior to serving.

Michelangelo

"A man paints with his brains and not with his hands." – Michelangelo

Michelangelo di Lodovico Buonarroti Simoni, known as Michelangelo, was an Italian sculptor, painter, architect, and poet. He was born in the Republic of Florence in 1475 and died in 1564. He never married and did not have any children, and there is little information about his private life.

David is undoubtedly the most famous of Michelangelo's sculptures, if not one of the most famous sculptures in the world. It symbolizes bravery, the story of a man who took down a giant with just a slingshot, the representation of courage and brilliant artistry. At 17 feet (5.2 meters) tall, almost the size of a 2-story building, *David* weighs 120,000 pounds (54 kilograms). Michaelangelo carved the statue out of a single marble slab instead of joining separate pieces. It took 40 men 4 days to move the statue half a mile from Michelangelo's workshop to the Piazza della Signoria. In 1873, *David* was moved indoors to the Galleria dell'Accademia to protect it from weathering. It is still located in this museum today.

Between 1498 and 1499, Michelangelo created the *Pietà,* considered a key work of Italian Renaissance sculpture. A French Cardinal commissioned the statue as a funeral monument, a Carrara marble sculpture depicting the Virgin Mary holding the dead body of Christ just after his crucifixion. In addition to being technically perfect, this representation of the Virgin is distinguished by her youthful features; it is also the only work Michelangelo signed – he carved

"Michelangelo Buonarroti, Florentine," on the sash running across Mary's chest. It was reported that Michelangelo later regretted his outburst of pride and swore never to sign another work of his hands. Today, it is honored in St. Peter's Basilica in the Vatican.

Michelangelo's most famous work is the Sistine Chapel ceiling inside the Vatican Museum. Visited by over 20,000 people daily, the Sistine Chapel ceiling was commissioned to Michelangelo in 1508 by Pope Julius II. At first, Michelangelo wasn't enthusiastic about painting the frescoes in the Sistine Chapel, as he thought of himself as a sculptor. *The Creation of Adam* is probably the most famous fresco in the Sistine Chapel and one of the most famous in modern art. It was created by Michelangelo around 1511. Michelangelo decided to represent the divine breath of life with God's and Adam's fingers almost touching each other.

Michelangelo spent 18 hours a day working on the Sistine Chapel – a piece that took him 4 years to complete – just the ceiling frescos. At 18 hours a day, 7 days a week over 4 years adds up to 26,208 hours of work. This work was physically demanding; he had to crane his neck and strain to reach the canvas. The time, pressure, and physical strain took a toll on his health.

One of the greatest artists of all time, Michelangelo Buonarotti died at 88 years old and is buried in the Basilica of Santa Croce in his hometown of Florence, Italy.

Carnevale

Carnevale is celebrated throughout Italy with colorful parades, floats, typical carnival foods, and fun events for children and adults. The Carnival dates change each year and are just over two weeks long. The last eight or nine days are the most eventful and most crowded. "Carnevale," from the Latin words "carne" and "vale," means "farewell to meat" in Italian, reflecting the pre-Lent timing. During the 40 days of Lent, parties were forbidden, and meat, sugar, and fats were off-limits. Carnevale in Italy takes place before Ash Wednesday, a last hurrah and a way to finish all rich food and drink stores before Lent. It is an occasion for sweet pastries, usually some sort of fritter dusted in sugar, easy to cook and easy to eat as you stroll the streets. Though these fritters have different names in different regions—chiacchiere in Lombardy, cenci in Tuscany, and frappe in Rome—they're all essentially the same dessert.

According to Venetian tradition, Venice's carnival started in 1162, when townspeople celebrated a victory over the Patriarch of Aquileia. In 1296, an edict from the Senate of the Republic declared the Carnival of Venice a public holiday. Some three million people gather each year to attend Carnival in Venice, an explosion of colors with confetti, masks, parades, floats and cheers.

Historically, masks were worn to conceal identities, allowing the classes to unite and celebrate without judgment. Today, many wear the traditional costume of the Bauta, which consists of a white mask called Larva, worn under a black tricorn, and by a dark coat, the so-called Tabarro. Masks are a form of artistic expression, and many unique, elaborately decorated masks are created. Costume contests and elegant masked balls are part of the festivities. Although Venice holds the most famous Italian carnival events, there are parades with spectacular floats and festivals almost everywhere. It is a time to celebrate and party, with music and dancing in the streets.

Where do you want to

travel next?